The Basic Essentials of
KAYAKING
WHITEWATER

by Bill Kallner &
Donna Jackson

Illustrations by
Cyndi

ICS BOOKS, INC.
Merrillville, Indiana

THE BASIC ESSENTIALS OF KAYAKING WHITEWATER

Printed in U.S.A.

Published by:
ICS Books, Inc.
One Tower Plaza
107 E. 89th Avenue
Merrillville, IN 46410

ACKNOWLEDGEMENTS

The authors would like to thank all the people who participated, directly and indirectly, in the creation of this book. Special thanks go to photographer Sandee Gerbers, to Whitewater Specialty instructors Pat McCabe, Dave Farin and Mike Wild, and to all of the students and instructors who've added their own special contributions to our teaching techniques.

Library of Congress Cataloging-in-Publication Data

Kallner, Bill.
   Whitewater kayaking: the basic essentials of / by Bill Kallner
and Donna Jackson.
     p.   cm. -- (The Basic essentials series)
   ISBN 0-934802-54-8 : $4.95
   1. Kayaking. 2. White-water canoeing.   I. Jackson, Donna, 1958-
   II. Title   III. Title: White water kayaking. IV. Title: Basic
essentials of whitewater kayaking.
GV783.K35   1990
797.1'22--dc20   90-31322
                                                 CIP

TABLE OF CONTENTS

1. EQUIPMENT:
THE TECH-WIENIE CHAPTER

You don't have to be a minor god with superhuman strength to enjoy the exciting and challenging sport of whitewater kayaking. We mere mortals can learn to paddle safely, skillfully, confidently and with control. Control is the key word here. It takes good paddling technique, good river-reading skills, good equipment and good judgment to achieve control in a rapid. Those are the basic essentials of kayaking, and that's what we cover in this book.

Whitewater recreational kayaks are as different from touring kayaks as downhill skis are from cross-country skis. In theory, you can ski downhill on cross-country equipment, and you can navigate a rapid in a touring kayak. In theory. In practice, the type and model of kayak you select can make a huge difference in how easily you learn and how well you paddle. So can the length of the paddle. And the fit of your lifejacket can be a help or a hindrance to your safety on the river.

Some of the most common problems entry-level kayakers face come from using inappropriate equipment. Whether you buy new equipment or used, seek advice from a knowledgeable whitewater outfitter. If budget constraints keep you from getting an absolutely ideal outfit, you'll at least be better able to make informed decisions on which equipment compromises you're willing to accept.

In the meantime, here's a general look at equipment for the sport.

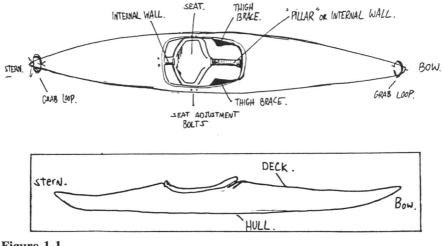

Figure 1-1
Kayak anatomy

Kayaks

Whitewater playboats are designed for one purpose — playing in rapids. They're designed to be highly maneuverable, but the features that make them easy to spin into and out of eddies usually reduce their ability to track (go straight) on the flat stretches of the river. Whitewater playboats give you lots of incentive to develop a clean, efficient forward stroke: You can learn to make a boat go straight, but you can't make a barge slip through tight spots or turn on a dime.

To make choosing a kayak more confusing, different models of whitewater playboats are designed not only with general performance characteristics in mind but also for paddlers of different sizes. The 110-pound woman who tries to paddle her 200- pound friend's whitewater kayak is often frustrated by the boat's unresponsiveness. It's not the boat or the paddler at fault. It's just a poor fit. Get a whitewater playboat that's the right size for you. Ask specific questions about the optimum paddler weight for the models of boats you're considering. Then try the boat on. You "wear" a kayak, so check the fit.

Finally, select a kayak constructed of tough, durable materials. Not too many years ago, most whitewater kayaks were made of fiberglass-and-resin composites. These days, plastic is more prevalent. While plastic playboats are not necessarily indestructible, plastic requires little maintenance and generally stands up well to the abuse paddlers give their boats in rapids.

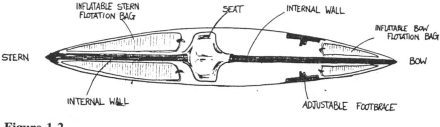

Figure 1-2
Kayak outfitting

Outfitting

Few whitewater kayaks are truly river-ready without some outfitting. Check the following standard outfitting details carefully. Some manufacturers use different types of outfitting systems; ask how they compare to these basic standards. In short, make sure the outfitting is up to your safety standards in any boat you paddle.

SEAT. In some kayaks, the seat component helps add rigidity and contributes to the structural integrity of the boat, which is an important safety consideration. If the seat has been altered, the safety and integrity of the boat may be compromised in certain whitewater situations. However, you may need to make minor adjustments in seat position. In many boats, it's a simple matter to loosen screws on either side of the cockpit to move the seat slightly forward or slightly back to get a better "fit" in your boat or to correct your weight distribution if you're running "bow-heavy" or "stern-heavy."

And if your hind end slips around in the seat, you may need to install some padding so you don't slip right out at a crucial moment. A simple way to do that is to tape foam to the sides of the seat so it hugs your hips. Duct tape is commonly used for this. Remember, though, that any time you change your seat outfitting you should practice a wet exit (which we'll explain in Chapter 2) to make sure you can still get out of the boat quickly.

FOOTBRACES. Kayaking is not just an upper-body sport. You'll use your legs far more than you may now imagine. The footbraces installed in the sidewalls of a boat help you "lock" yourself in and help keep you from sliding forward when going over steep drops. Adjust the footbraces so that when your legs are extended in front of you with your knees slightly flexed, the balls of your feet rest comfortably on the pegs.

THIGH BRACES. If you're in an appropriately sized boat and your footbraces are properly adjusted, your knees should be cocked slightly toward the outside edges of the boat and your thighs should fit in the thigh braces. If your proportions are somewhat different than those of the ideal paddler the boat designer had in mind, you may need to make some minor adjustments. Move the seat slightly forward if your legs are short, or back if your legs are very long, until you can "grip" the thigh braces with your thighs; adjust the footbraces accordingly. Just make sure your seat adjustment doesn't leave you bow-heavy or stern-heavy when you get the boat in the water: If you have to move the seat that much to get good contact in the thigh braces, the boat may not be an appropriate size for you.

Most kayakers pad the thigh braces to make them more comfortable and better-fitting. Inexpensive pre-cut foam pads are available from most kayak dealers, or you can cut your own. Install the pads with a flexible waterproof contact cement.

INTERNAL WALLS. The internal walls or "pillars" positioned along the centerline of the boat provide structural support for the deck. The walls are an important safety feature: If a boat with an unsupported deck becomes pinned in a rapid, the water pressure can cause the deck to collapse on the paddler's legs, trapping him or her in the boat. Internal walls help support the deck so there's enough clearance for the paddler to get out. Minicell foam is usually the material of choice for internal walls because of its light weight and stiffness, and because it absorbs less water than other types of foam. Foam can also be notched out if you need to create heel wells in the wall to keep your feet from cramping.

FLOTATION. While the internal walls generally provide enough flotation to keep a swamped kayak from sinking to the bottom of the river, you'll want to install additional flotation in your boat. Inflatable flotation bags help displace more water. In the case of a capsize, the kayak floats higher, it's easier to rescue and it's less likely to suffer damage from being wrapped around a rock. In short, properly secured flotation bags are a cheap form of insurance for your investment in a boat.

GRAB LOOPS. Loops of nylon webbing or rope should be mounted on both ends of the deck. The loops give a swimmer an easy-to-grasp handle.

Kayak Fit Checklist

1. What is the optimum paddler weight range in this model of kayak? Are you in that range?

2. Are you "sloppy" or sliding from side to side in the seat?

3. Can you adjust the footbraces so that when your legs are extended in front of you (knees slightly flexed) the balls of your feet rest comfortably on the pegs?

4. In that position, are your knees cocked toward the outside edges of the boat?

5. Do your thighs fit into the thigh braces when you're in that position?

6. Are you comfortable?

Paddles

Do yourself a favor. Get knowledgeable advice to make sure you buy a paddle that's in the right size range for you. Then buy a GOOD paddle. Paddles are made of wood or synthetic materials. There are good wood paddles and cheap wood clubs; there are good synthetic paddles and there's junk. It can take a long time to beat up a paddle you hate enough to justify getting a decent stick. So bite the bullet right from the start and plan to spend about $140 on a decent paddle.

The shaft should feel comfortable in your hands — not too large in diameter and not too heavy to keep stroking. Expect a decent paddle to have an ovaled shaft in the grip areas; the oval "memory" helps you keep track of where the blades are. The blades should be offset or "feathered" at an angle of 80 to 90 degrees.

Kayak Paddle Sizes

Your height is one factor to consider in choosing an appropriate paddle size, but body stature (shoulder width, torso length, etc.), type of boat, blade size, paddling style and the nature of the rivers you paddle should also influence your choice of paddle length. Here are a few general guidelines:

PADDLER HEIGHT	PADDLE LENGTH
5'0" to 5'4"	196-200 cm
5'4" to 5'6"	200-204 cm
5'7" to 5'9"	202-206 cm
5'10" to 6'0"	204-206 cm
Over 6'	204-210 cm

This is to reduce wind resistance on the blade that's out of the water when you're taking a stroke with the other blade. Look for a paddle with curved or dihedral blades. Flat blades are also available, but they don't give you the extra power or efficiency of a curved or dihedral shape.

Finally, are you right-handed or left-handed? Right-hand control (RHC) paddles are more readily available, and many schools and clubs teach everyone right-handed technique. This puts some leftys at a disadvantage and can lead to developing some nasty habits to compensate for the awkwardness. If you're a lefty, you may want to get started with a cheap flat-blade paddle, which you can use either left-handed or right-handed. Just promise that once you pick a control hand you'll get a better curved or dihedral blade paddle in either right-hand control or left-hand control (LHC).

Lifevests

Buy a good-quality Type III U.S. Coast Guard-approved vest-type PFD (personal flotation device). A vest-type PFD does more than help keep your head above water. In addition to buoyancy, it provides warmth for your torso in cold water, and it helps protect your body from bumps and bangs. Buy the smallest size that fits comfortably. Loose and baggy may be fashionable in other garments, but your life can depend on having a snug-filling PFD that won't ride up and come off over your head in rough water. Buy one that fits, then remember to put it on and zip it up.

Helmets

A helmet is required. Put it on at the beginning of your river trip, and don't take it off until the end. Helmets probably prevent more serious head injuries in people walking around on slippery river banks than in people floating upside-down in their kayaks. And remember that if you take it off at lunch and it bounces off the rock and disappears, you'll probably spend part of the afternoon floating upside-down in your kayak needing that helmet. Look for a helmet that fits snugly but is comfortable enough to wear all day, and that offers adequate protection for your forehead, temples and the nape of your neck.

Sprayskirts

The neoprene sprayskirts whitewater kayakers wear around their waists seal around a boat's cockpit rim to keep water out. Sprayskirts are available in different cockpit sizes, so make sure you get one that fits your boat. They also come in different waist sizes, and should fit snugly around your torso. Gather up a handful of the neoprene when pulling the skirt on to avoid stressing the material.

Clothing

Start with the assumption that you'll be getting wet. Often. Sometimes it's just the wet from paddle drip, which can feel like Chinese water torture on cold days if you're not dressed for it. Other times you catch a cold wave full in the chest. Then of course there are times when your eskimo roll won't work and you'll be well and truly dunked in the river.

And then there are those glorious, beautiful, sunny summer days. On a warm day on a warm river, you may need nothing more than a swimsuit and footwear. Forget your barefoot beach look — you need protection for your feet that absolutely will not come off if you take a swim. Traditional starting-out footwear is a pair of old sneakers, but here's the downside: Worn-out soles offer poor footing on slippery river rocks, and some sneakers inhibit your entry and exit from the boat. A better choice is a pair of mesh-top "water socks" for warm weather or wetsuit booties for any type of weather.

One of the best investments you can make in river clothing is a paddling jacket. A good jacket will help keep wind and spray from robbing you of body warmth. Look for a jacket made of coated nylon fabric with neoprene closures at the neck and wrists. On cool days, layer the jacket over clothes that will help keep you warm even when wet, like polypropylene and synthetic pile.

Wear clothing that will help protect you from hypothermia, which is a potentially deadly drop in the body's core temperature. On cold days or on cold rivers, you may need a wetsuit or drysuit. A wetsuit traps a thin layer of water next to your skin to act as an insulating layer. A drysuit seals out water to reduce heat loss. Neither is a guarantee against hypothermia, but either will buy you valuable time to get yourself to safety.

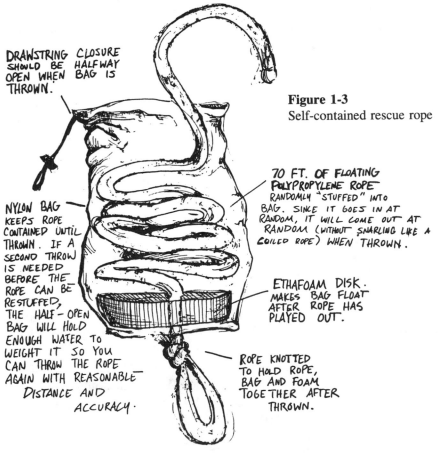

DRAWSTRING CLOSURE SHOULD BE HALFWAY OPEN WHEN BAG IS THROWN.

Figure 1-3
Self-contained rescue rope

70 FT. OF FLOATING POLYPROPYLENE ROPE RANDOMLY "STUFFED" INTO BAG. SINCE IT GOES IN AT RANDOM, IT WILL COME OUT AT RANDOM (WITHOUT SNARLING LIKE A COILED ROPE) WHEN THROWN.

NYLON BAG KEEPS ROPE CONTAINED UNTIL THROWN. IF A SECOND THROW IS NEEDED BEFORE THE ROPE CAN BE RESTUFFED, THE HALF-OPEN BAG WILL HOLD ENOUGH WATER TO WEIGHT IT SO YOU CAN THROW THE ROPE AGAIN WITH REASONABLE DISTANCE AND ACCURACY.

ETHAFOAM DISK. MAKES BAG FLOAT AFTER ROPE HAS PLAYED OUT.

ROPE KNOTTED TO HOLD ROPE, BAG AND FOAM TOGETHER AFTER THROWN.

Rescue Rope

We think it's every paddler's responsibility to carry a rescue rope and know how to use it. This is a skill we teach on the first day of our beginner-level classes (before doing a river trip), and one we review in more advanced classes. We'll cover this skill in Chapter 6.

Eyewear

If you wear glasses, wear eyeglass restraints. If we knew of a foolproof way to keep eyeglasses from fogging up after rolling, we'd tell you. As it is, index-finger windshield wipers are the best defogger we know. Contact lens wearers may need to wear their glasses while working on the basics; it helps to be able to open your eyes underwater to check your positions. Neoprene visors are great for shading your eyes, or keeping rain off your glasses.

Noseclips

Remember, kayaking is a gravity sport. Every time you're upside down (like when practicing your eskimo roll), gravity will suck a few gallons of water into your sinuses. Life's too short. Get some swimmer's noseclips and put them on anytime you think you might tip over. Just do it.

2. GETTING WET

Before you put on your noseclips and head for the river, plan to spend some time in quiet water working on some basic skills. An indoor pool is fine if the weather is cold, but nothing beats a beach with a nice sandy shoreline. At the beach, work through the progression of skills we present in this chapter — how to get into a kayak, the tuck, the wet exit, the important "C-to-C" motion and the eskimo rescue. You should be comfortable with these skills before moving on to Chapters 3 and 4, which cover paddling strokes, braces and the eskimo roll.

Do yourself a favor: Follow the progression! This book is based on the sequential learning approach we use in our paddling school. Remember how you learned the alphabet before you learned to read? The basic skills we present in this progression are as important to kayaking as the ABCs are to reading. Take time to master the basics, and it will be easier to learn more difficult skills later.

Stretch Out

The first thing we do on the beach or shore before getting into a kayak is stretch out. Stretching helps warm the muscles and reduce muscle strain as you position your body in what, at first, may seem like some pretty weird positions. Remember, in kayaking you'll value flexibility more than brute strength, and stretches help your flexibility. We suggest you stretch out in the lifevest, sprayskirt and helmet you'll be wearing on the water.

Getting Into A Kayak

Position the boat parallel to the shoreline in shallow water, and put your paddle shaft on the back rim of the cockpit. In this position, you can learn to use the paddle as an outrigger to help stabilize the boat as you get in. Stand facing the bow of the boat with the shaft of the paddle against the backs of your calves. Hold the paddle shaft against the back rim of the cockpit, leaving a butt-sized space between your hands. Slide your bottom boatward, and sit on the deck just behind the cockpit — right on top of your paddle shaft. Lift your legs into the boat, one leg at a time starting with the leg nearest the boat. Put your feet right in front of the seat and keep your knees bent. When both feet are in, support your weight on the paddle, maintaining contact between the paddle shaft and the back of the cockpit rim, while you lift your buttocks, straighten your legs and slide your feet forward. Sit down and get your feet positioned on the footpegs and your thighs in the thigh braces.

Now move the paddle in front of you and rest it on the deck. The next step is sealing the cockpit with your sprayskirt. The sprayskirt is worn with the long part of the skirt hanging in front of your knees; the chimney should be pulled up under your pectoral muscles, and you wear your lifevest on top. Reach behind you and pull the back of the skirt over the cockpit rim. Working from back to front, pull the stretchy shock-cord or rubber gasket over the rim. Get someone to help hold the skirt in place if you have trouble getting it on alone until you've had some practice. If it's really tough to stretch it into place, try getting the skirt wet before getting into the boat.

Make sure the grab loop on the front of your sprayskirt is on the topside of the spray deck once everything is sealed. This is the "quick-release" handle you'll need to "pop" the skirt off the cockpit when you bail out. Always check to make sure your sprayskirt grab loop is where it should be. Make it a habit — EVERY TIME you get into the boat — to be sure your sprayskirt grab loop is not caught in the cockpit seal.

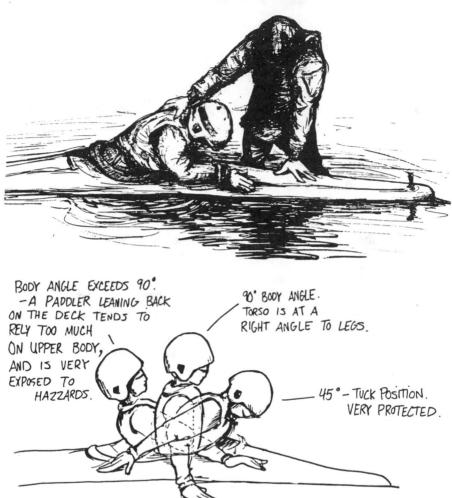

BODY ANGLE EXCEEDS 90°.
—A PADDLER LEANING BACK
ON THE DECK TENDS TO
RELY TOO MUCH
ON UPPER BODY,
AND IS VERY
EXPOSED TO
HAZZARDS.

90° BODY ANGLE.
TORSO IS AT A
RIGHT ANGLE TO LEGS.

45° - TUCK POSITION.
VERY PROTECTED.

Figure 2-1
Practice assuming the protected tuck position until it becomes an automatic
response.

The Tuck

Get settled back in the boat, get your sprayskirt sealed, and
get a friend to help you through the next few steps. For now, throw
your paddle up on shore and stay in water just deep enough to float
you.

The first thing to do any time you tip over in your kayak is
tuck your body into a protected position. Bend forward at the waist
as if you were going to kiss the deck in front of you. Imagine
you're in your kayak, floating upside-down over a rocky riverbed.

If you were to sit up straight with your torso at a 90 degree angle to your legs, you'd be pretty exposed to those rocks. To reduce your exposure, learn to get into the tuck position right away. Then if you do float over a rock before you can wet exit or roll up, your lifevest or helmet can absorb the impact.

While you're still right-side-up, practice getting out of the kayak. These are the motions you'll use in the wet exit.

Grasp the sprayskirt grab loop and pull it straight out away from the cockpit to break the seal, then up to lift the skirt away from the rim.

Plant the heels of your hands on the sides of the boat next to your hips, as if the boat were the arms of a chair and you were going to lift yourself out of it. Relax your legs to release them from the footpegs and thigh braces. Keeping your legs straight, bend forward at the waist and lift your bottom out of the seat and onto the deck just behind the cockpit. Imagine you're flying off the high dive in the pike position. When we work on this motion upside down in the wet exit lesson, gravity will help you get the idea.

The Wet Exit

Have a friend take you into water 3 to 4 feet deep. As you practice the wet exit, your friend's job is to stay alert and help if you have any problems. Your friend can either spin the boat right-side up with you in it, or support your body with his hands so you can get your face to the surface for a breath of air.

Time to get wet! Take a deep breath, tuck, and tip over. Stay in that tuck, and reach up with your hands. Wave to your friend, slap the bottom of the boat with your hands, and count to 10 slowly. The 10-count gives you time to open your eyes, get your bearings, and get used to hanging out upside down while staying tucked.

Now pop the seal on your sprayskirt like you practiced earlier. Put your hands on the sides of the boat next to your hips, and relax your legs to release them from the footpegs and thigh braces. Think of it as "taking off the boat" like you would take off a skirt or pair of trousers. Keep your legs straight and roll forward in the pike position as gravity helps pull you out of the seat. Don't try to swim to the surface until your feet have cleared the cockpit. Trying to "climb" out with your legs will just make you feel tangled up.

Relax, keep your legs straight and let gravity do its job; when your feet are clear, then you can swim to the surface and swim your boat to shore.

Practice the wet exit with a friend until you feel comfortable with the whole process before moving to the next skill.

The "C-To-C" Motion

The "C-to-C" motion is a technique for moving a kayak (with you in it) from upside-down to right-side-up. It gets its name from the C-shaped curve of your spine. When the boat is upside-down, you form a C facing one direction; to get the boat right-side-up, you form a C facing the other way.

Have a friend help you practice this skill. In this exercise we use the bow of a second kayak, but you can have your friend hold a lifevest or other buoyant object in place of the second boat.

To begin practice of the C-to-C motion, get in your kayak and have your friend take you and the second boat into water 3 to 4 feet deep. Sit up straight and think about where things are: The hull of your boat is flat on top of the water. Hold your hands straight out in front of you, palms down. Have your friend hold the second boat perpendicular to the left of your kayak. Tuck forward, then roll out to your left, moving your hands to the deck of the second boat and laying your head on your hands. Your hands are merely there to support you and keep your face from getting wet the first time you practice the C-to-C motion.

Using your hands only for gentle support, turn your kayak upside down. (Fig. 2.2a) Keep the angle of your torso in relation to your legs less than 90 degrees. Visualize your spine forming a backwards letter C.

Without pushing down with your hands, use your abdominal muscles and legs to turn your kayak back right-side-up. Keep your head on your hands and press your lower leg up into the thigh brace. Visualize your spine forming a letter C facing the opposite direction as before. Roll back into the tuck position, keeping your head down. (Fig. 2.2b)

Throughout the C-to-C motion, keep the angle of your torso in relation to your legs less than 90 degrees. If your body angle becomes greater than 90 degrees, you'll find yourself exposed to more hazards (review the lesson on The Tuck) and you'll find yourself grunting and straining your upper body to move the boat when you should be doing it with the C-to-C motion.

Practice these steps with a friend until you can do them perfectly yourself. Go through each step slowly and smoothly so your friend can check your performance using the C-to-C Checklist below. Correct any problems before moving on. Then practice on the other side.

After you master the motion keeping both hands on the deck of the second boat, work on getting more and more of your body wet as you practice the C-to-C motion. Use only one hand to support yourself on the deck of the second boat; turn your kayak upside down with the first C, turn it back right-side-up with the second C, roll back into your tuck and keep your head down.

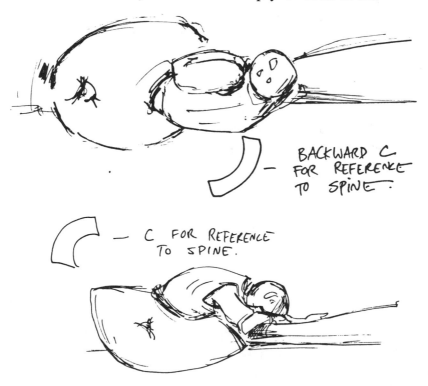

BACKWARD C FOR REFERENCE TO SPINE.

C FOR REFERENCE TO SPINE.

Figure 2-2
The C-to-C motion, a technique for moving a kayak from upside-down to right-side-up, is an important element of skills presented later.

C-To-C Checklist

1.   Is the angle of your torso in relation to your legs less than 90 degrees throughout the motion?

2.   When you form the first C, is the hull of the kayak facing the sky?

3.   Are you turning the boat right-side-up by forming the second C with your spine? A common problem is that the paddler tries to "muscle up" by pushing down with his hands on the second kayak instead moving the boat with the C-to-C motion. This problem is especially likely to occur if you lean back, making the angle of your torso in relation to your legs greater than 90 degrees.

4.   As you right the boat with the second C motion, are you rolling back into the tuck position and keeping your head down?

The Eskimo Rescue

The eskimo rescue is a technique for using the aid of a second kayaker to go from upside-down to right-side up. Suppose you tip over in a river situation: You could wet exit and swim to shore. But if another kayaker in your party is nearby, he could paddle over and position the bow of his kayak where you could reach it. And you could reach up and use the bow of that boat to right yourself just like you did while practicing the C-to-C motion. Pretty slick.

If you've been following the progression, you've already learned everything you need to perform this technique except for the communication signals. Communication is important, because when you're upside-down underwater you can't call your companions with a jolly, "By golly, I could use some assistance," and you can't see where that assistance might come from. So we practice non-verbal signals for aid and how to "look" for assistance with your hands.

For the first few times you practice the eskimo rescue, have a friend stand in the water and move the bow of a second kayak within your reach.

To begin this practice session, put on your noseclips, take a deep breath, tuck and roll over. Keeping your body in the tuck position, reach up with your hands and slap the bottom of the boat three times — loudly! This is the signal for aid.

"Look" for assistance with your hands: Holding your hands perpendicular to the boat, run them back and forth along the mid-section of your kayak. In this practice session, your friend will move the bow of the second kayak to the midsection of your boat and bump it gently against your hand. Reach up and put your hands on the deck of the second boat. Keep your head down and curve your spine in the first C position, with the boat upside down. Take a moment to check your position: If you've "leaned back" and the angle of your torso in relation to your legs is more than 90 degrees, close up that angle.

Move your body into the second C position to put the kayak right-side-up. Remember, don't push down on the second boat with your hands: Use the C-to-C motion to move the boat.

Roll back into the tuck position, keeping your head down. You've just completed an eskimo rescue.

Practice this exercise on both sides.

3. THE STROKES

For most of Chapter 2 we had you leave your paddle on the shore. Now that you know how to wet exit properly if you tip over, get your paddle so you can begin to work on strokes. Kayaking strokes are used for two basic purposes — propulsion and steering. In this chapter we'll cover how to move forward, how to put on the brakes, and how to "steer", which includes making quick, snappy U-turns. We present only the pure forms of essential strokes at this level. Many stroke variations are used in paddling, but the material in this chapter will give you a solid foundation on which to build. First, though let's establish the most basic skill — how to hold the paddle properly.

How To Hold The Paddle

Grasp the paddle shaft in your dominant or control hand, which we will assume for now is your right hand: Circle the shaft, wrapping your thumb under the shaft. The flat part of the back of your right hand should be parallel to the surface of the water. Without changing your grip on the shaft with your right hand, loosely circle the shaft with your left hand, placing your left hand about a shoulder-width away from your right and holding the paddle symmetrically. Your left thumb should be wrapped under the shaft and the back of your left hand should be nearly parallel to the surface of the water. But think of your hands as having different tasks: Your right hand will control the paddle. Your left hand will merely help support the paddle for the moment.

BASELINE RIGHT
WRIST POSITION.

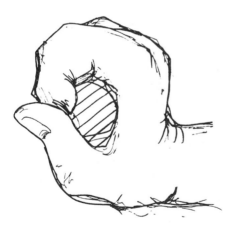

RIGHT WRIST COCKED BACK.
MOVE LEFT BLADE INTO POSITION
PERPENDICULAR TO SURFACE OF
WATER —

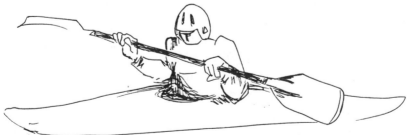

Figure 3-1
Cocking the wrist of your control hand back moves the offside blade into position
for a stroke.

Now focus on the blades. The blades of a kayak paddle sort of act like a swimmer's hands. When a swimmer uses the forward crawl stroke, his hands are slightly curved and the concave palm side of the hand "catches" the water. Similarly, when a paddler uses a forward stroke he uses the curved side of the kayak blade to "catch" the water. We'll call this curved or concave side of the paddle the power face. Orient the right blade so it is perpendicular to the surface of the water, with the power face (the concave side) oriented toward the stern of the boat and the backface (the convex side) oriented toward the bow.

If you're using a flat-blade paddle, orient the blade on your right side as described above and designate the blade surface facing the stern as the power face. Use duct tape, waterproof athletic tape or waterproof marker to create a visual reference point on this face of the blade to help make sure you're using the proper side as you perform the strokes covered in this chapter.

With the right blade oriented as described above, look at the left blade: When the right blade is perpendicular to the surface of the water (ready to "catch" the water in a forward stroke), the left blade is nearly parallel to the surface of the water. If you tried to take a forward stroke with the left blade in this position, it would slice through the water without "catching". To take an effective stroke on your left side you'll have to change the orientation of the left blade.

In making that change, DO NOT let the shaft rotate in your right hand. Maintain your grip on the shaft with your right hand, but let the shaft rotate in your left hand. Cock your right wrist back as if you were gunning a motorcycle, letting the shaft rotate in your left hand. Now grip the shaft in your left hand, and the power face of the left blade should be perpendicular to the surface of the water and ready for a forward stroke on your left side. To take a stroke on your right, you would simply return your right wrist to its original position, letting the shaft rotate in your left hand.

Practice this motion out of the water, watching the blades, until it feels natural.

Hold the paddle symmetrically in front of you, bend your elbows and bring your hands to your shoulders; your hands should be shoulder-width apart. While some kayakers, particularly racers, position their hands much farther apart on the shaft of the paddle, the wider stance for entry-level recreational whitewater kayakers is not recommended. The shoulder-width hand position lessens a paddler's vulnerability for shoulder injuries. If you find your hands creeping into the wider stance, wrap narrow strips of waterproof athletic tape around the shaft on either side of where each hand should be to maintain that shoulder-width stance. Those visual and tactile reference points on the shaft will help remind you to position your hands in the more protected position.

Translation For Lefties

To use your left hand as your control hand, grasp the shaft with your left hand first, allowing the shaft to rotate in your right hand. Orient the left blade so it is perpendicular to the water; the right blade should be parallel to the surface of the water. To change the orientation of your right blade, cock your left wrist back. The following stroke descriptions are oriented to right-hand-control paddlers. We hope they're easier to translate than knitting directions.

The Forward Sweep

The first stroke we'll work on is the forward sweep, a steering stroke that helps you turn the boat while maintaining forward momentum. We teach this directional stroke first for two reasons. First, turning is exactly what a whitewater kayak is designed to do, so it's a fairly easy stroke to learn. Second, this stroke will give you a good introduction to torso rotation, which is an important component of other strokes you'll learn. Torso rotation helps you use the muscles in your abdomen and back, which are larger and more powerful than the muscles in your arms. In paddling, consider your arms merely connectors between the shaft of the paddle and the large muscles in your torso. In this sport, that's the key to strength without steroids.

Push yourself out into shallow water and let your paddle float beside you for a moment. Sit up straight, tall and proud in your boat. If you slouch or lean back against the cockpit rim (a terrible habit!), you lose the use of those large torso muscles and you overuse your arms. Sit up straight, face forward, and make sure your knees and feet are properly braced. Without shifting your

Figure 3-2
The forward sweep uses the power face of the blade, a low shaft angle and torso rotation.

lower body, rotate your torso to one side until your shoulders are nearly parallel with the centerline of the boat. This is the torso motion you'll use in the forward sweep. Try rotating to the other side too before you pick up your paddle.

To begin the forward sweep, slice the right blade of your paddle into the water as close to the boat and as far forward as you can reach without leaning forward or "hinging" at the waist. Watch the blade to be sure the power face is in position to "catch" a full face of water as you sweep. (Illust. 3.2a)

As you rotate your torso, picture your paddle as the sweep-second hand on a clock ticking from 12 to 6. The shaft of your paddle as it sweeps in this wide arc should be at a low angle in relation to the water, closer to horizontal than to vertical. Watch your blade angle, making sure the power face is positioned to catch water throughout the sweep.

As you rotate and your paddle sweeps, the bow of the boat will turn away from the stroke. Remember the laws of motion? "For every action there is an equal and opposite reaction." As you sweep on the right, the boat will react by turning in the opposite direction — to the left. (Illust. 3.2b)

At the end of the stroke, slice the blade out of the water, tilting the top edge of the blade slightly toward the boat and cutting it out of the water. Practice the forward sweep on your right side, spinning the boat in a circle, until you master the motion.

To practice the forward sweep on your left side, cock your right wrist back to put the power face of the left blade in a position to "catch" the water, and sweep counterclockwise from 12 o'clock to 6 o'clock. Again, the bow of the boat will turn away from the stroke — this time to the right. (Illust. 3.2c)

Follow the blade with your eyes and keep your shoulders parallel to the paddle shaft as you rotate your torso and sweep the paddle in a full arc all the way from 12 o'clock to 6 o'clock. Following the blade with your eyes helps remind you to complete the torso rotation to perform a full 180-degree sweep. The phases of the stroke nearest the ends of the boat provide the greatest turning momentum in the stroke. Make sure your sweep arcs a full 180 degrees when you perform this stroke.

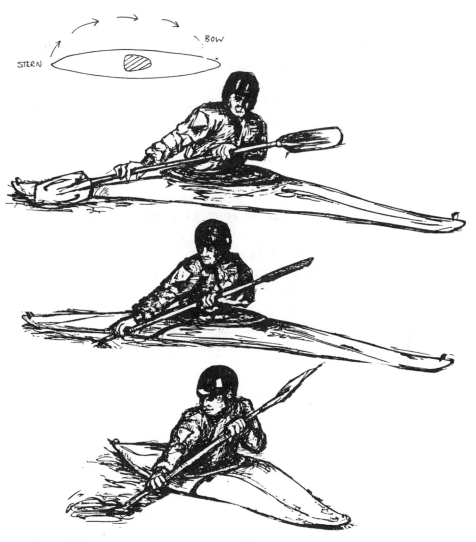

STERN

BOW

Figure 3-3
The reverse sweep uses the backface of the blade, a low shaft angle and torso rotation.

The Reverse Sweep

While the forward sweep moves the bow of your boat away from the stroke, the reverse sweep moves the bow toward the stroke. To begin the reverse sweep, rotate your torso so your shoulders are nearly parallel with the centerline of the boat. Slice the right blade of your paddle into the water near the stern as close to the boat and as far back as you can reach without learning back against the deck.

Use the backface of the blade to "catch" the water. Follow the blade with your eyes as you rotate your torso sweeping the blade from 6 o'clock to 12 o'clock. Again, as the shaft of your paddle sweeps in this wide arc it should be held low and as close to horizontal as possible. As you rotate and your paddle sweeps, the bow of the boat will turn toward the stroke — to the right. At the end of the stroke, slice the blade out of the water. Practice the reverse sweep on your right side, spinning the boat in a circle, until you master the motion. Practice on both sides.

The Forward Stroke

The forward stroke is a propulsion stroke. Alternating forward strokes on your right and left sides should propel your kayak straight ahead. Should. It isn't quite as easy as it sounds. Remember those pesky laws of motion? Those "equal and opposite" reactions? The design features that make a whitewater kayak easy to turn make it very reactionary — and keep it from going straight unless you MAKE it go straight.

Before we move on with the forward stroke, think back to the forward sweep. Got that stroke down? Remember why you use it — to turn the boat? Good. Use the forward sweep when you want to turn the boat, but NOT when you want to make the boat go straight. We want to make this point clear. One of the worst habits you can develop is putting a little sweep in your forward stroke. Etch this in your memory: The forward and the forward sweep are two totally different and distinct strokes which should be used for two totally different purposes.

As you practice the forward stroke, keep an eye on your shaft angle. If the shaft is at a low angle in relation to the water — closer to horizontal than vertical — you're sweeping. In a proper forward stroke, the shaft will be closer to vertical.
(Fig. 3.4)

To get in position for a forward stroke, sit up straight and hold the paddle out in front of you, keeping your elbows slightly bent and pointed down toward your sprayskirt. Twist at the waist so your right shoulder points toward the bow and the right blade is near your right foot. Without changing your grip on the paddle, move the back of your left hand to your forehead. Adjust the angle

Figure 3-4
The forward stroke uses the power face of the blade, a nearly vertical shaft angle
and torso rotation.

of the right blade so it's perpendicular to the boat and you can see the power face, and slice the blade into the water next to your foot.

Punch forward with your left hand without pulling it down or back toward your left shoulder; the blade will "catch" the water. At the same time, "unwind" your torso and feel the boat move forward toward the paddle. This is a good time to remember that your arms are merely connectors between the shaft of the paddle and the large muscles in your torso. This is the power phase of the strokes. Make sure the blade is fully immersed and that it "catches" before you begin to unwind your torso.

The power phase ends when the blade is just past your hip. If you tried to continue past this point, you'd just be "lifting" water, not powering forward. Slice the blade straight up and out of the water. Now look at the shaft: It should be nearly horizontal, with both blades out of the water. Think about your body position: Your torso should be rotated, "wound up" with your left shoulder pointing toward the bow, and in position to begin a stroke on your left side.

Move the back of your right hand to your forehead and adjust the left blade so it's perpendicular to the boat and you can see the power face. Slice the left blade into the water near your left foot.

Punch forward with your right hand without pulling it down or back toward your right shoulder; the blade will "catch" the water. At the same time, "unwind" your torso and feel the boat move forward toward the paddle. Again, this is the power phase of the stroke. End the power phase when the blade is just past your hip and slice the blade straight out of the water. You should be back in position now for another stroke on the right.

If you're rotating your torso properly to channel the power of the larger muscle groups into your stroke, at the end of a stroke on one side you'll always be in position for a stroke on the other side. As you paddle forward, practice making strokes of equal length and equal strength on each side; this helps you go straight.

Beware of a tendency to pull on the blade during the power phase of the forward stroke. The power should come from torso rotation, not from dragging the blade through the water. If your arms are getting tired, you're probably bending your elbows and pulling the blade through the water.

The Back Stroke

Beginning paddlers rarely use the back stroke for propelling themselves backwards (that'll come later!). But this stroke can save your hide when you've propelled yourself enough and you need to slow down, stop the boat, or maintain your position in the current while you figure out which way to go. This is an important stroke, and you want to be able to count on it when you need it. So learn to do it properly: The back stroke should not look, feel or function like the reverse sweep. They're two entirely different strokes and are used for entirely different purposes.

To get in position for a back stroke, hold the paddle in front of you, elbows slightly bent, with the shaft horizontal. Twist at the waist, drawing your right shoulder back toward the stern; as you rotate your torso, move the whole paddle to your right so it's nearly parallel with the boat.

Adjust the angle of the right blade so it's perpendicular to the boat and push the blade into the water behind your right hip, catching the water with the backface of the paddle. At the same time, adjust the angle of the shaft to a more vertical than horizontal position. While we cautioned you against pulling the blade through the water during the power phase of the forward stroke, you do need to push the blade through the water on the back stroke. Still, remember to "unwind" your torso to give some real power to your push.

The power phase of the back stroke ends when the blade is as far forward as you can comfortably reach without leaning forward at the waist; the shaft should still be fairly vertical. Slice the blade out of the water by moving the shaft to a more horizontal position. Twist at the waist again, drawing your left shoulder back toward the stern and moving the left blade into position for a stroke.

Adjust the angle of the left blade so it's perpendicular to the boat and push the blade into the water behind your hip, catching the water with the backface of the paddle. At the same time, adjust the angle of the shaft to a more vertical than horizontal position. Unwind and push.

Again, end the power phase when the blade is as far forward as you can comfortably reach without hinging, and slice the blade out of the water by moving the shaft to a more horizontal position. As you backpaddle, practice making strokes of equal length and equal strength on each side.

Figure 3-5
The draw stroke uses the
power face of the blade
and a nearly vertical shaft
angle to "sideslip" laterally.

When you feel comfortable with the back stroke, try this exercise: Paddle straight forward, building up a good head of steam, and then slam on the brakes as smoothly as you can with back strokes. Try to keep your boat straight.

The Draw Stroke

With the draw stroke, you can move a kayak laterally — literally drawing the boat toward the paddle blade. This steering stroke is unlike any kind of steering you would do in a car, but it's useful on the river when you want to "sideslip" around an obstacle in your path (like a boulder) without changing the direction your bow is heading. (Fig. 3.5a,b)

Here's basically what happens in a draw stroke: The paddler rotates toward the direction in which he wants to move the boat, planting the paddle blade on that side in the water with the power face of the blade in the water parallel to the boat. The paddler "catches" the water with the power face and draws the boat toward the paddle. The paddler must stop the stroke when the blade is about 6 inches from his hip; if not, the boat will continue to move toward the paddle and he'll draw the boat right over. People tip over sometimes while learning these strokes, so now might be a good time to review the progression on the wet exit — especially if you skipped that chapter.

One of the things that often bewilders students is how to get the blade in the water in the starting position for this stroke. The easiest way to explain on paper is by describing an exaggerated exercise; once you start doing the stroke the entry phase will begin to feel natural.

Here's the exaggerated exercise: To get the paddle in the water for a draw to the right, begin by holding the paddle in front of you with your elbows bent. Cock your right wrist back to put the right blade parallel with the surface of the water. Without letting go of the paddle, wipe the back of your left hand across your forehead from left to right; as you do this, keep your left elbow pointed down toward your sprayskirt. Now twist at the waist, facing your right, and "sight down" the shaft of the paddle, along the power face and to the tip of the right blade. Plunge that tip into the water straight out from your hip, at the same time punching out with your left hand until both hands are over the water, the paddle shaft is vertical and the blade is immersed with the power face facing the boat. The blade is now in position to begin a conservative draw stroke.

You won't do the weird wiping-your-forehead and sighting-down-the-shaft stuff every time you start a draw stroke. The point of the exercise is simply to help you position the paddle, plunge and punch. Now you're ready to "catch" the water with the power face and draw the boat toward the paddle.

As you become more comfortable with the motion it takes to get in position to begin the stroke, start reaching out farther to your side before slicing the blade into the water. This reach may seem radical, but as you draw the boat toward the paddle the stroke helps support you and keeps you right-side-up despite your reach — as long as you keep your weight centered in the boat.

Once you learn to reach out confidently as you begin the draw stroke, you'll see how much one draw can move the boat. But suppose you're moving downriver straight toward R.I.P. Rock: You reach out and plant your best draw. The boat moves toward the paddle, but not far enough to pull you around R.I.P. Rock. Jumpin' Jupiter, you need to do another draw stroke! Your paddle blade is still in the water, right where you stopped the stroke about six inches from your hip. So let's talk about an in-the- water recovery to position your paddle for another draw.

Figure 3-6

The In-The-Water Recovery.

1. Power face "catches" water and boat is drawn toward blade.
2. Power phase ends.
3. Cock lower wrist forward to turn blade perpendicular to boat and ...
4. Slice the blade edge-first straight out through the water perpendicular to boat.
5. Cock lower wrist back to put the power face back in position to "catch" water for the next draw.

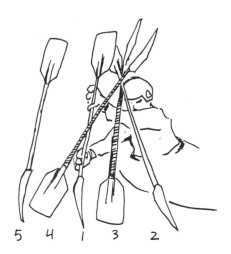

Think about the blade in the water. The power face, which you used to "catch" the water during the stroke, is parallel to the boat. If you just pushed away with the blade to get it back where the stroke began, you would negate the dynamite draw stroke you just completed. Instead, cock your wrist forward to turn the blade perpendicular to the boat, slice the blade edge-first out through the water, then turn it back so you can "catch" water on the power face for another stroke. (Fig. 3.6) The real trick to this recovery is to make each phase of the motion separate and distinct but smooth.

Practice the draw stroke with the in-the-water recovery on both your right and left sides. Then get a friend to help you with an exercise: Have your friend sit in a kayak or stand in the water, and paddle straight toward him. Just before you ram him, your friend will pick a direction and point to your right or left. Draw in that direction to move off your collision course.

The Duffek Stroke

The draw stroke used the power face of the paddle to "catch" the water straight out from your hip, and the boat moved laterally. The Duffek stroke also uses the power face; in this stroke you "catch" the water with the power face oriented toward your bow, holding the blade in a fixed or "static" position while the boat moves around it in a snappy U-turn. Why would you want to make a U-turn? In the middle of a rapid there are calm spots called eddies. As you're heading downstream, you can pull out of the main current by doing a U-turn (or eddy turn) into one of these calm spots. Then

31

Figure 3-7
The Duffek uses the power face
of the blade to "catch" the water.

you can catch your breath, look around and figure out where the heck to go from there.

To set up for a Duffek stroke on your right side, hold the paddle in front of you, elbows bent and pointed down toward your sprayskirt. Check your hand position on the shaft — your hands should be shoulder-width apart. Without changing your grip on the paddle, move your left hand in front of you and rest it on your right shoulder. You should be able to see the power face of the blade. Move the paddle into and out of this position until it feels natural.

Since this is a static stroke in which the boat must be moving to work, have a friend help you discover how this stroke is supposed to feel. Position the paddle, keeping it just above the surface of the water. Have your friend stand in the water and give your kayak a shove. Lower the blade into the water at the 3 o'clock position. (Sometimes you'll "close up" the insertion angle, but the Duffek stroke never begins with the blade behind your body.) As you slice the blade in, the power face will "catch" the water. (Fig. 3.7b)

The boat will start a snappy turn as soon as the blade catches. The boat moves around the paddle in this stroke, so don't confuse things by trying to move the paddle once it's in the water. Lean the boat into the turn, keeping your weight centered in the boat. The paddle will help support you as the kayak moves around it. Keep your left hand on your right shoulder and the paddle in the same position as your bow turns toward the power face of the blade in the water. (Fig. 3.7c)

To stop the turn, level out the boat, roll your right wrist forward to change the blade angle and go into a nice, smooth forward stroke.

Have your friend give you another shove, and try this motion on your left side. Practice with the "push me" method until you feel comfortable leaning into the turn.

Then thank your friend, and be responsible for your own momentum. Use forward strokes to get the boat moving, put your paddle in the Duffek position, slice it into the water, lean into the turn as the bow moves toward the blade, then stop the turn with a forward stroke. Practice on both sides.

Make sure your paddle is properly oriented so the power face can "catch" the water. If you use the backface instead, the stroke turns into a poor imitation of the reverse sweep. Try that trick on the river, and instead of making a snappy turn into Last Chance Eddy you may push yourself away from it and right over the edge of Killer-Fang Falls.

Two-Faced Reminder

In each of the strokes covered in this chapter, it's important to "catch" the water with the correct face of the paddle. Check yourself.

When using the strokes forward, forward sweep, draw, and Duffek use the power face. For the backstroke and reverse sweep use the backface.

4. ROLLING & BRACING

Be honest: Did you turn to this chapter first, flipping past everything else to get right to the eskimo roll? If we had a dollar for every paddler who thought the eskimo roll was the single most important skill in kayaking, we'd stop buying lottery tickets. We don't mean to imply it isn't useful; it is. Above all, the roll is a powerful confidence-builder. But the roll is what you use when everything else has gone wrong and you're upside down.

If you haven't done so already, please work through the progression of skills we presented in the previous chapters. Each of those skills is every bit as important as the roll. Some are important when you want to stay right-side-up. Others are components of the roll.

There is one variation in the progression that we don't mind: If you want to skip ahead to the section on bracing and save the roll for later, that's fine. While the roll is what you use when all else fails and you've tipped over, the high brace is what you use to keep from tipping over. We only present the eskimo roll first in this chapter because many of our students get rolls right away by following this progression. The roll comes in handy when they tip over while practicing braces.

The Eskimo Roll

In this section, we assume you've followed our earlier progression — that you're in a properly-fitted kayak, that you tuck like a pro, and that you've got the C-to-C motion down pat. Any time you get stuck, stop and go back to the last step you could perform perfectly. Master each step before moving on.

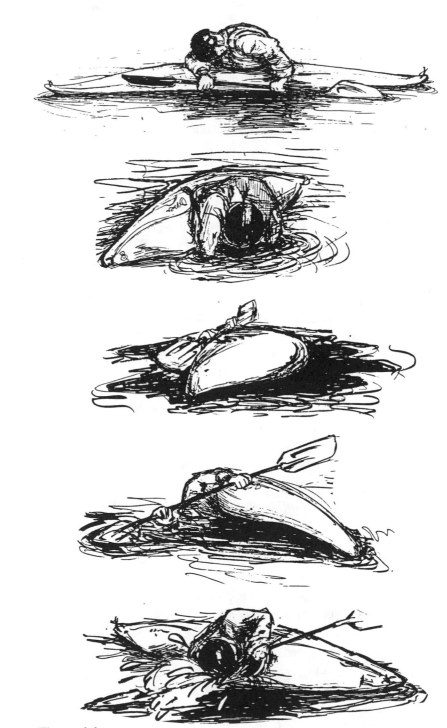

Figure 4-1
The Eskimo Roll uses the C-to-C motion to right an upside-down boat.

Before we break the eskimo roll down into its component parts, let's take a quick look at what we're working toward. For now, just look — don't try. Trust us. You'll have more success if you wait and go through the progression step by step. We only present this look at the whole to help you understand the sum of the parts. (Fig. 4.1)

The paddler starts by tucking, and he positions the paddle at his side. He tips the boat over. Now he's upside down, with the paddle in the set-up position. As he moves into the first C position, he moves the paddle perpendicular to the boat. He uses the blade to help support him as he moves into the second C position, turning the boat from upside-down to right-side up. When the boat is upright, he can sit up.

Get a friend to help you practice in ankle-deep water. Holding the paddle in the normal paddling position, rotate to your left to put the paddle shaft parallel with the boat. Roll your right wrist forward until the right blade is parallel with the surface of the water, with the power face up. Without changing the paddle position, lower yourself onto your right shoulder. Move into the first C position, at the same time swinging the paddle out to your right and keeping it above the surface of the water until the paddle is at a right angle to the boat. Look at the right blade: It should be parallel to the surface of the water with the power face down. Now move into the second C position to turn the boat upright; your paddle should do nothing more than provide a little support as you move into the second C position to right the boat. Tuck forward to center your weight. Now you can sit up. Practice this sequence until it feels natural to move the paddle as you do the C-to-C motion.

Move into deeper water for the next exercise. Put your paddle in the set-up position and have your friend lower you over, supporting your shoulder. Have your friend smack the bottom of the boat to signal you to move into the first C position as you swing the paddle perpendicular to the boat. Have your friend smack the bottom of the boat again to signal you to move into the second C position, using the paddle blade for as little support as possible as you use the C-to-C motion to right the boat. When the boat is upright and stable, lean forward and center your weight before sitting up. Practice this sequence. When everything works perfectly, have your friend support your shoulder a little farther underwater and practice the sequence again.

In the exercise above we have a friend signal you to move from C to C by smacking the bottom of the boat. This helps remind you to break down the motion into component parts, rather than muddling them all together. Work to make the motions smooth and integrated, but remember that each individual component is important.

The last exercise included all the parts of the roll except tipping over. This time, move the paddle into the set-up position and tip over without having your friend support your shoulder. Have your friend smack the bottom of the boat to signal you to swing the paddle out and move into the first C position, then smack it again to move into the second position to right the boat. Lean forward to center your weight and sit up. That's the eskimo roll.

The eskimo roll is one skill we won't have you practice on both sides at this level of learning. Work on the roll only on your dominant side for now.

The High Brace

As we said earlier, the high brace is what you use to keep from tipping over. The irony of the situation is that you're almost guaranteed to tip over while practicing the high brace. That's because you have to simulate almost tipping over before the brace means much to you. When you do end up upside-down, the first thing you should do is tuck. Then attempt an eskimo roll, thump the bottom of your boat to request an eskimo rescue from another paddler, or wet exit.

Before you start working on the high brace, go back to Chapter 2 and review the C-to-C motion. The two have a lot in common. Say a big wave just hit your kayak: You feel yourself in the first C position as the boat is tipping over. If you could move to the second C, you could put your boat back in a stable, upright position. The high brace is a technique for using your paddle to help support your weight as you move into the second C.

Balance and body position are critical here. You want to keep your weight centered over the boat. Practice keeping your weight centered. Without using the paddle, tip the boat up on one side.

Keeping your body upright, balance the boat on edge with your body in the first C position and your weight centered. Practice balancing like this then leveling the boat out by curving your spine the opposite direction into the second C. Practice on both sides.

Now move your paddle into the brace position at a right angle to the boat. The blade on the side you're going to tip toward should be parallel to the surface of the water with the power face down. Your elbows should be pointed down toward your sprayskirt. Balance the boat on edge again, keeping your elbows down (under the paddle shaft) and your weight centered. Feel the first C. Ready? Let the boat tip just a liiiiiiiiiiittle farther. When you feel like you're going to lose it, brace the blade lightly on the surface of the water to help support you as you move to the second C position and level out the boat. Practice on both sides. Keep your elbows down. Your elbows should never be higher than the paddle shaft in the high brace.

As you become more comfortable with the high brace, let the boat tip farther and farther. Work to reduce the amount of pressure you put on the bracing blade as you move from C to C to right the boat. As you practice, watch your bracing blade: Keeping your head in a position where you can see the blade encourages you to keep your head down and will help you center your weight in the boat, which will help you reduce your reliance on the blade.

Eventually you should be able to brace up even when the boat is nearly upside-down. Keep working to reduce the amount of pressure you put on the blade. The blade is just there to help support you as you move the boat from upside-down to right-side up with the C-to-C motion.

Don't lean back. If the angle of your torso in relation to your legs is greater than 90 degrees, you won't be able to move the boat upright with the C-to-C motion. If you're putting a lot of pressure on the bracing blade to get up, try leaning forward.

After practicing on both sides until this all seems quite natural, get a friend to help you (pick this friend carefully). This friend will be your "river simulator". On the river, who knows if you'll tip to the left or the right? On the lake, you can practice reacting with a brace on the appropriate side by closing your eyes and having your friend tip you from side to side without warning.

Figure 4-2
Use the C-to-C motion in the high brace. You can help level the boat by pulling
your lower knee up into the thigh brace.

5. EDDY TURNS, PEEL-OUTS & FERRIES

Before you head for the river to try out the techniques you've learned so far, let's look at how to use them. In this chapter we'll show how to work with the features of a rapid and apply the strokes you practiced in Chapter 3 to perform basic paddling maneuvers — eddy turns, peel-outs and ferries. With these maneuvers, you'll be better able to break down a rapid into do-able parts to control your progress down the river. But before you can use the features of the river to work with, not against, the water, you must learn to "read" the river.

Remember that kayaking is a gravity sport. Water flows downstream because of gravity. As it flows, it's affected by several factors — gradient, volume, current speed and obstacles. Gradient refers to the downhill slope of the riverbed over which the water flows. Volume refers to the amount of water in a given space, and generally is measured in cubic feet. The current speed or rate at which it flows is measured in cubic feet per second (cfs), and is the result of the combined effects of gradient and volume. The obstacles water hits as it flows downstream give a river its general character, and that character is influenced by the variables of gradient, volume and current speed.

Obstacles

Let's focus on the obstacles. To a whitewater paddler, obstacles aren't barriers. On the contrary, obstacles create the river features we use to achieve control in a rapid.

The most common obstructions are rocks and boulders and irregularities in the shoreline. Rocks so deep you can't even see them can still have an impact on the surface of the water; for example, a standing wave can form just downstream. Other rocks lie just barely under the surface: From upstream, the smooth sheet of water flowing over a "pillow rock" is barely discernable. Finally, there are rocks you can see above the surface of the water; an important feature called an eddy forms on the downstream side.

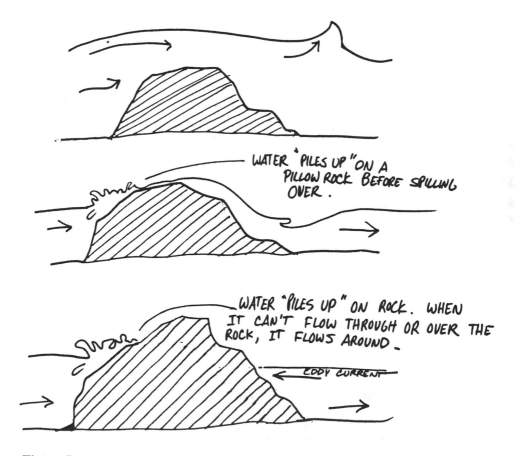

WATER "PILES UP" ON A PILLOW ROCK BEFORE SPILLING OVER.

WATER "PILES UP" ON ROCK. WHEN IT CAN'T FLOW THROUGH OR OVER THE ROCK, IT FLOWS AROUND.

EDDY CURRENT

Figure 5-1
As water flows downstream, it's affected by obstacles like rocks and boulders.

In an eddy, the current actually flows upstream in relation to the main current. (Fig. 5.2) When the downstream current hits the obstacle, a cushion of water piles up on the upstream side. If the water can't flow over or through the obstacle, it has to flow around. Water always seeks the path of least resistance, so as it spills around the rock it starts to fill in the empty space on the downstream side. This creates the eddy current, which is strongest just downstream from the rock. Eddy lines form where the fast downstream current collides with the water flowing upstream in the eddy.

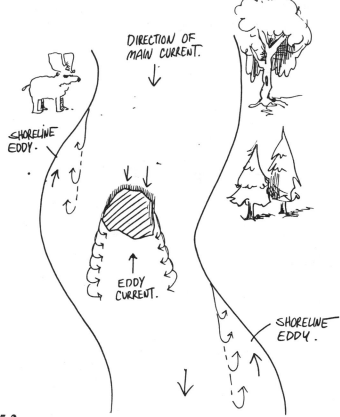

Figure 5-2
Eddies offer opportunities to get out of the fast downstream current.

The V-shaped eddy lines help you "read" the water in a rapid. There's a rock at the upstream "point" of a V; even if it's a pillow rock just under the surface, the point of the V will tell you the rock is there. And just as the V-shaped eddy lines help show where the obstacles are, they also help show the channels between obstacles. The Vs that point downstream generally indicate the route between the rocks.

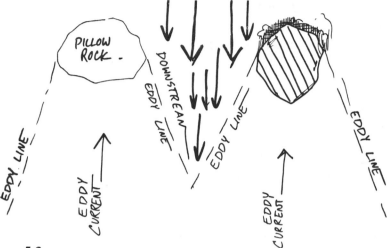

Figure 5-3
A "downstream V" indicates a path between obstacles.

People who "shoot the rapids" usually do nothing more than try to keep the bow pointed downstream and follow the downstream Vs to the bottom of the rapid. These people usually have only one rule: Don't lean upstream. Remember the cushion of water that piles up on the upstream side of an obstacle? When a kayak gets turned sideways in the current, it becomes an obstacle to the current. If you lean your boat and/or your body weight upstream, the water will pile up on that edge. Faster than you can say "Ninja Current" it will build up pressure over a large enough surface area to flip the boat upstream.

If, on the other hand, you keep the boat leaned slightly downstream, you'll offer less surface area for the current to hit. A downstream lean allows the water to flow under the boat, and doesn't present a hard edge or wall to catch the water.

The downstream lean becomes particularly important when you get turned sideways in the current and the current pushes you toward a rock. An instinctive reaction is to lean away from any scary thing that looms up in front of you. That's the equivalent of leaning upstream, though, and will quickly ensure that things go from bad to worse. Instead, lean the boat toward the rock. The cushion of water piled up on the upstream side of the rock will work in your favor: Ride that cushion and work yourself around the rock. If you come off with your bow facing downstream, great. If you come off stern-first, that's not the end of the world. At least you're not upside-down. Keep in mind that the boat is pointed on both ends, and you won't be the first person to run a rapid backwards.

Forwards or backwards, it's far more fun and much safer to "play through" a rapid than to just "shoot it" from top to bottom. Most of the time you can't see a whole rapid from the entry point. Scouting from shore may help, but sometimes what you can't see from shore comes as a real surprise as you paddle through the rapid. The basic rule of whitewater is this: Never paddle past the last safe landing point you absolutely, positively can reach. In the next section we'll introduce a maneuver you can use to reach those last-chance landings.

The Eddy Turn

To pull out of the fast current and enter the relative calm and security of an eddy, you do a U-turn called an eddy turn. This maneuver harnesses the energy of two opposing currents — the downstream current and the eddy current — to pivot the boat.

So how do you get from facing downstream in the main current to facing upstream in the eddy? The maneuver has three essential components — angle, momentum and lean.

Angle refers to the angle at which the kayak crosses the eddy line, exposing the bow of the boat to the strongest upstream current in the eddy while the stern remains exposed to the downstream current. (Fig. 5.4) It's important to cross the eddy line as close to the rock as possible, where the eddy current is strongest. The necessary degree of angle varies, depending on the speed of the current, but is generally 45 degrees or more.

Momentum is the forward power needed to drive the bow across the eddy line so the two opposing currents can pivot the boat — without driving the boat straight through the eddy and out the other side.

Figure 5-4
The eddy turn uses the energy from two opposing currents to spin the boat 180 degrees.

Lean refers to the way you must lean into the turn, just like you would on a bicycle. As you drive the boat across the eddy line, exposing half the boat to eddy current, you must adjust your lean. Remember which way eddy current flows? To maintain a downstream lean in that type of current you have to lean into the turn; it will only look like you're leaning upstream to someone who doesn't know you've moved into current flowing the opposite direction as the main current of the river.

You'll notice we haven't even mentioned using a paddle. Your prime concerns should be angle, momentum and lean. With the right angle, the correct amount of momentum and a good lean into the turn, the water will do the work to spin the boat 180 degrees. You use your paddle only to position your boat to enter the eddy at the appropriate angle, to produce adequate momentum to drive the bow across the eddy line, to support your lean and to stop the turn at 180 degrees so you don't spin right out of the eddy. The

strokes you'll use — the forward sweep, the forward stroke, and
the Duffek — were covered in Chapter 3.

Here's how the eddy turn should look when you put all the
pieces together: Say you're heading downstream and decide to pull
into an eddy on your left. There are no obstructions between you
and that eddy. You want your bow to enter the eddy where the
eddy current is strongest (just downstream of the rock), but with
enough clearance that your boat won't bang into the rock as it
pivots. Paddle toward the eddy, steering to adjust the angle so the
boat will be at about a 45 degree angle to the eddy line as the bow
enters the eddy. As the bow starts to cross the eddy line, do a full
forward sweep on your right to help start the turn while maintaining
the momentum needed to push you across the eddy line.

By this time your feet should actually be in the eddy. Lean
the boat into the turn, keeping your body centered but tilting the
boat to "lean downstream" in the eddy current. At the same time,
move your paddle into the Duffek position and slice it into the
water about 3/16 of an inch downstream of the rock (where the
eddy current is strongest) with the power face of the blade perpendicular to the eddy current. (Fig. 5.5) Hold on as the boat moves
around the paddle, accentuated by your lean and the forces of
downstream current moving your stern while eddy current moves
your bow. When your kayak has spun a full 180 degrees and you're
facing upstream in the eddy, level out the boat and turn your Duffek
into a short forward stroke to stop the turn and hold you in the
eddy. Now you can look over your shoulder to see what's downstream, and to pick out your next eddy.

*Before you attempt this or any other maneuver in moving
water, study the safety principles in Chapter 6.*

Maneuvers like the eddy turn take practice. Practice involves
making mistakes and correcting them. If at all possible, have an
experienced instructor coach you. But also get used to coaching
yourself. When you miss an eddy, try to figure out why so you
can correct the problem next time. Here are some common problems:

● *Trying to turn in the downstream current.* If the boat is still
in the downstream current and you "lean into the turn," you're
almost sure to flip. You have to drive the bow across the eddy line
so the two opposing currents can pivot the boat. Wait to plant your

Figure 5-5
Plant the Duffek in the strongest
part of the eddy, lean into the
turn and hold on as the boat
spins around the paddle.

Duffek stroke until the boat starts to carve its turn and you can reach the strongest part of the eddy with your paddle. Be sure you plant your Duffek stroke in the strongest eddy current, not in the downstream current.

● *Too little angle.* We said earlier that it's important to cross the eddy line as close to the rock as possible, where the eddy current is strongest. But if you cross the eddy line with too little angle, the water spilling around the rock will deflect your bow away from the eddy. The angle of the boat in relation to the eddy line should be at least 45 degrees as you drive the bow into the eddy.

● *Trying to set the angle too far from the eddy.* You don't have to establish your entry angle half a mile upstream. If you try to, what usually happens is the current pushes you away from the eddy; we'll explain how this works when we get to the backferry. Aim right for the rock creating the eddy, and use your steering strokes to adjust your position and angle just before you drive the boat across the eddy line.

● *Hitting the eddy too low.* The farther away from the rock you are when you enter the eddy, the weaker the eddy current will be. Again, it's important to cross the eddy line close to the rock where the stronger eddy current is so the two opposing currents can do the work of pivoting the boat.

● *Leaning your body, not the boat.* Keep your weight centered as you lean the boat into the turn.

● *Leaning the boat the wrong way.* If you lean away from the turn, the eddy current will pile up on the edge of your boat and flip you. Lean the boat into the turn.

● *Improperly executed Duffek.* If you use the backface of the blade instead of the power face to "catch" the water when you plant your Duffek, the stroke will turn into a poor imitation of a reverse sweep; you can push yourself right out of the eddy. Remember, the Duffek uses the power face to "catch" the water.

● *Forgetting to stop the turn.* Once the boat is spinning, your 180-degree turn can easily become a 360-degree turn and you'll spin right out of the eddy. Turn your Duffek into a short forward stroke to stop the spin and hold you in the eddy.

The Peel-Out

The eddy turn is the U-turn maneuver you use to pull out of the fast current into the relative calm of an eddy. The peel-out is the U-turn maneuver you use to get back in the game! It takes you from your temporary resting place in the eddy, where you're facing upstream, and pivots the boat 180 degrees as you re-enter the main downstream current.

Angle, momentum and lean are key components of the peel-out as well as the eddy turn. And like the eddy turn, the peel-out uses the energy of two opposing currents to pivot the boat.

Here's how the peel-out works: You're sitting in an eddy facing upstream. To pivot the boat, you need to get the eddy current moving your stern toward the rock creating the eddy as the downstream current moves your bow the other way. To get the most push from the eddy current, exit the eddy where the current is strongest — as close to the rock as you can pass with enough clearance to keep from banging your stern on it as the boat pivots. You'll need a burst of momentum to drive your bow across the eddy line, so you may need to back up in the eddy so you can take a couple of quick forward strokes — not forward sweep turning strokes but pure, straight-ahead-momentum forward strokes. Get the boat moving, then use a steering stroke to position it to cross the eddy line at about a 45-degree angle.

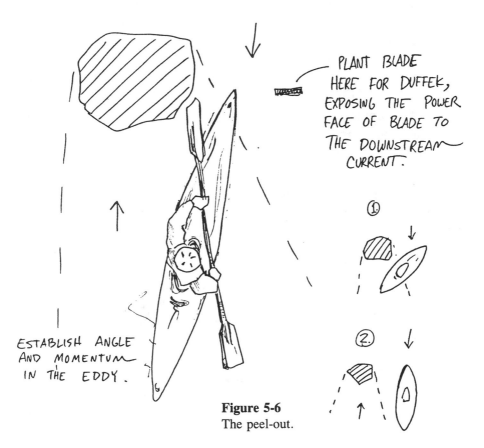

PLANT BLADE HERE FOR DUFFEK, EXPOSING THE POWER FACE OF BLADE TO THE DOWNSTREAM CURRENT.

ESTABLISH ANGLE AND MOMENTUM IN THE EDDY.

Figure 5-6
The peel-out.

As your feet cross the eddy line and the boat moves into the faster downstream current, lean the boat downstream, keeping your weight centered. Support your lean with a Duffek stroke on your downstream side, slicing it into the water with the power face of the blade perpendicular to the downstream current. Hold on as it "catches"; the boat will move around the paddle, accentuated by your lean and the forces of eddy current moving your stern while the faster downstream current moves your bow. When your kayak has spun a full 180 degrees and you're facing downstream in the main current, level out the boat and turn your Duffek into a short forward stroke to stop the turn.

Here are some common problems with the peel-out:

● *No momentum.* Even if your angle and lean are perfect, without momentum to "punch" across the eddy line you won't escape the eddy. The second the tip of your bow crosses the eddy line the downstream current will push it, all right — right along the eddy line so you end up still in the eddy and facing downstream. Get the boat moving.

● *Leaning your body, not the boat.* Keep your weight centered as you lean the boat into the turn.

● *Leaning the boat the wrong way.* If you lean away from the turn, the downstream current will pile up on the edge of your boat and flip you upstream. Lean the boat into the turn. Lean downstream.

● *"Muscling" the Duffek.* This is most often a problem with paddlers who try to use upper-body strength — instead of angle, momentum and lean and letting the opposing currents turn the boat — to pull the boat around. The Duffek should merely help support your lean and accentuate the turn.

● *Too little exit angle.* If you cross the eddy line with too little angle, you'll be in position for a ferry, not a peel-out. The angle of the boat in relation to the eddy line should be at least 45 degrees as you drive the bow out into the downstream current.

Ferries

Ferries are paddling maneuvers that let you move your boat across the river — from bank to bank, eddy to eddy, channel to channel — without moving downstream. Ferries are useful for getting yourself where you can better scout a section of river, or positioning yourself to run a section. They can even be used to work your way upstream.

There are two types of ferries: In an upstream ferry, you face upstream and use forward strokes. In a backferry, you face downstream and use backstrokes. In both types of ferries, you point the upstream end of the boat in the direction you wish to go and use angle, momentum and lean to let the water do the work.

How does the water do the work to move you across the river without washing you downstream? Try this simple demonstration: Lay a fat, round magic marker on a smooth, level surface. Air currents behave very much like water currents, so you're going to provide the current. Point one end of the marker at about a 30-degree angle to the "current", take a deep breath and blow. The current will push the marker across the table. (Try it again with no angle; the "current" will flow around the marker without moving it at all.) When a boat is positioned at an angle to the current, the water will move it like the air current moved the marker or like the wind moves a tacking sailboat. However, you'll need momentum to counteract the current and keep the boat from drifting downstream as the water pushes you across the river.

The Upstream Ferry

Suppose you're sitting in an eddy facing upstream. You've looked over your shoulder: Hello, Killer-Fang Falls. The riverbank nearest you is a sheer rock wall 200 feet high. But on the opposite shore there's a nice, sandy beach and your friends are waiting for you to join the picnic. Unless you're Spiderman or you have a death wish, you need to get to the picnic. So you're going to use an upstream ferry.

Set your angle while you're still in the eddy; for now, put your boat at a 20-30 degree angle to the main current. Sometimes you'll need more or less angle: In mild current, you may need a 60-80 degree angle before the water can push the boat across the river. In strong current, you may need to decrease the angle to keep from getting "peeled out".

While you're still in the eddy, develop the momentum to carry you across the river without drifting downstream. Back up, if necessary, and use forward strokes to get the boat moving. Use a steering stroke, if necessary, to adjust your angle before you punch across the eddy line.

As your feet cross the eddy line, lean the boat (not your body) downstream. Maintain the boat lean as long as you're in the main current. Your angle, momentum and lean should put you in a position where you won't have to do another stroke — the water will do the work. But if you need to, you can use forward strokes to maintain your momentum and forward sweeps to adjust your angle. Never use a reverse sweep to adjust your angle on an upstream ferry; you'll kill your momentum.

When you cross the eddy on the other side of the river, adjust your lean; if you maintain the boat lean you used in the main current, you'll expose the edge of your boat to eddy current and tip over.

As you practice upstream ferries on the river, try this exercise. Find a spot with good eddies on either side of a current jet. Work to develop your angle and momentum in the eddy; try to ferry across the jet without using any additional strokes.

The Backferry

The backferry is most frequently used to move the boat from channel to channel rather than shore to shore. The basic idea is the same as the upstream ferry: Angle the upstream end (in this case, the stern) the direction you want to go and use angle, momentum and lean to get the water to move the boat.

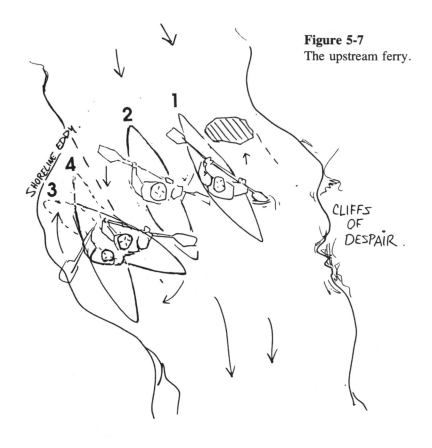

Figure 5-7
The upstream ferry.

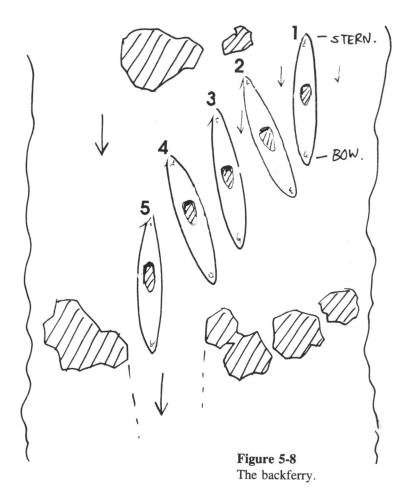

Figure 5-8
The backferry.

The biggest difference is that, at this level of learning, you'll seldom start a backferry from an eddy. Most of the times when you need to backferry, you'll already be facing downstream in the main current. Use reverse sweeps to adjust your angle, and back-strokes to keep the current from sweeping you downstream. Lean the boat downstream as long as you're in the main current, but remember to adjust your lean if you cross into an eddy.

6. PLAYING RAPIDS

In Chapter 5, we talked about eddy turns, peel-outs, upstream ferries and backferries, and how these fundamental maneuvers are used to control your progress through a rapid. In this chapter, we'll talk about a few more features of rapids, and what to do when things get a little out of control.

Horizon Lines

Looking downstream from your kayak, suppose you see what is called a horizon line. Beyond that smooth, watery horizon, the river is hidden. You see the tops of the trees that line the riverbanks, but not the tree trunks. Along with the roar of the water, a horizon line is a pretty obvious signal to find a landing point and proceed with extreme caution.

Not every horizon line signals a Killer-Fang Falls, though. Suppose you can see some frothy water just downstream of that smooth horizon line, and even though you can't see the riverbanks you can see parts of the tree trunks. Baby-Tooth Ledge may be a fun playspot — or it could be as deadly as Killer-Fang Falls. In the next section, we'll explain why.

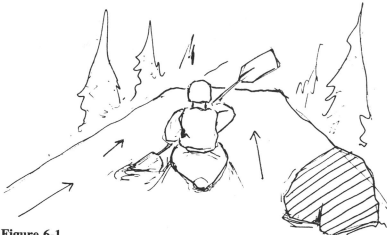

Figure 6-1
When you see a horizon line downstream, use eddy turns, peel-outs and ferries to maneuver to a safe stopping point where you can get out and scout or portage.

Holes & Hydraulics

Eddies aren't the only river features that have water flowing upstream in relation to the main current. Water can also develop a strong upstream current or "reversal" after dropping over a ledge. As the water flowing downstream drops over the ledge, it picks up speed — like a truck going down a steep grade. All that energy has to go somewhere, but it meets resistance when it hits the river bottom. Some of the water will flow out downstream, but much of it will "bounce" up off the bottom until gravity pulls it back down and it falls back upstream. Where this frothy, aerated recirculating water meets the smooth water flowing downstream, you'll see a visible depression or "hole" — a hole you can't dig yourself out of. If you put a buoyant object (like a kayak) into that hole, the two opposing currents (compounded by the force of gravity) would tend to hold it there.

The shape of the ledge or obstruction that creates a hole has a big effect on its character. The most dangerous type of hole is formed by a very smooth, regular ledge or obstruction with no breaks or irregularities where the water can "flush" out. This type of hydraulic can be deadly; don't get anywhere near a manmade or natural feature like this, because there may be no way out. You can't escape upstream, and the recirculating "backwash" downstream wants to pull you back into the hole.

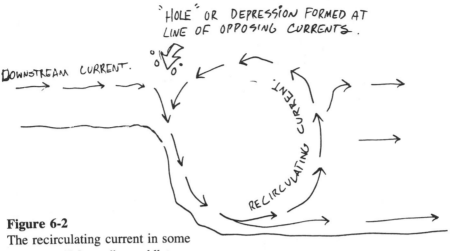

Figure 6-2
The recirculating current in some
holes can "Maytag" a paddler.

You can, however, escape out the ends of some holes, depending on their shape. If the ends of a hole point upstream, you don't stand much chance of escaping out the ends. You'd be trying to move upstream, uphill and against the current. But if the ends point downstream, there may be enough water flushing out the "corners" to let you break out of the hole.

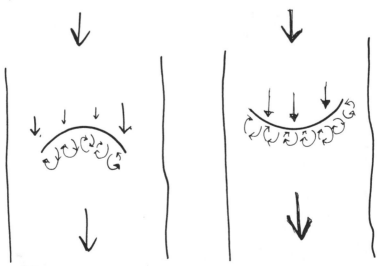

Figure 6-3
You stand a better chance of breaking out of the ends of a hole if they point downstream (left) than upstream (right).

Strainers

Not all obstructions disrupt the flow of water: Strainer, sweeper and sieve are regional names for trees that have fallen in the water. Like a tea strainer, liquids flow through and solids get caught. Avoid these like the plague: You don't want to get caught in the branches of a submerged tree with all the force of the downstream current to hold you there.

Undercuts

This is another type of obstruction that doesn't disrupt the flow of water as you would expect. In Chapter 5 we talked about how water normally behaves around obstructions like boulders: It can't flow through, so it piles up in a cushion on the upstream side of the boulder, then spills around the rock, creating an eddy on the downstream side. When a rock is undercut or altered in shape by the forces of nature, water may in fact be able to "flow through". To make matters worse, you never know if logs or other debris have been washed into the undercut and lodged there. A paddler who gets washed into an undercut may be trapped there by the force of the water. So stay clear of any boulder or obstruction that doesn't have a cushion of water on the upstream side or an eddy on the downstream side.

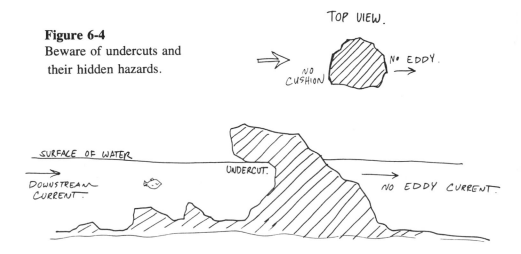

Figure 6-4
Beware of undercuts and
their hidden hazards.

Scouting A Rapid

Let's inventory what we've covered so far. We've introduced you to some of the river hazards you'll want to avoid, and shown how to use eddy turns, peel-outs and ferries to control your progress through a rapid. You're reaching a point where you're going to have to start making choices. Sometimes you'll choose the left channel over the right, or an upstream ferry over a backferry. But the basic choice you must make in each and every situation is this: Do I run this or portage? The choice is yours; don't ever let anyone

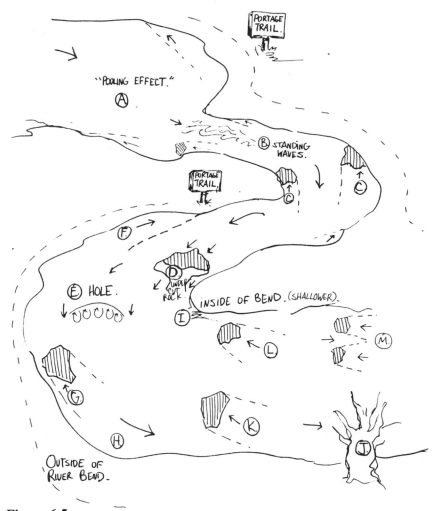

Figure 6-5
The choice to paddle or portage any rapid is yours and yours alone.

talk you into doing something you don't want to do or have no business doing.

When you get out to scout a rapid from shore, look at it from bottom to top; this gives you a perspective on what you'll have to deal with downstream if you choose to run it and make a mistake. When you "boat scout" without getting out of your kayak, remember the basic rule we discussed in Chapter 5: Never, ever paddle past the last landing point you absolutely, positively can reach. We're going to boat-scout the rapid in Fig. 6.5.

Above the rapid, the river is wide and slow. In the rapid, the riverbed narrows and gets steeper. The water flowing downstream meets resistance from the water trying to flow through the narrower space and "pools up" above the entrance to the rapid (Point A). You could backferry above the entrance to the rapid for a better look at the next section.

To understand the dynamics of the water where the riverbed narrows, think what happens when you put your thumb over the end of a garden hose: The amount of water flowing out won't change, but it sure seems to be moving faster and more powerfully as it spurts out around your thumb. The same sort of thing happens in constricted river channel: The amount of water flowing through the channel won't change, but all that energy has to go somewhere. Here it pushes the water up then gravity pulls it back down to form a series of standing waves (Point B).

Downstream of those standing waves, the riverbed widens out, the waves dissipate, and there are eddies you're sure you can hit on both sides of the river. If you decide to run those waves, keep the boat straight and the paddle in position to do a forward stroke or high brace. Then head for your target eddy (Point C), where you can get a better look at what's ahead before you move farther downstream. For an even better perspective, use an upstream ferry to get to the eddy on the other side for another look.

What you'll see ahead of you are two potential hazards. On one side there is a huge boulder with no cushion of water piling up on the upstream side (Point D). It could be undercut, so stay away from it.

On the other side you see a small horizon line, with frothy water bubbling up just downstream (Point E). Above it, there's a shoreline eddy where you could take out and walk around, if necessary (Point F). You're sure you can make it to that eddy, so you peel out and move downstream to that eddy.

From that position, you can see that the ends of the hole point downstream. If you got caught in that hole, you would probably flush out. So you decide to try running the hole. Peel out and position the boat so you'll hit the hole with the boat perpendicular to the line of opposing currents in the hole. You'll need a good head of steam to punch through that line of opposing currents, and you'll need to develop that momentum before you get to the hole. Paddle like hell, then as you punch through that line reach forward with good, strong forward strokes to pull the rest of your boat past the hole.

Once you're clear, do an eddy turn at Point G to get a better look at the rest of the rapid. As the river bends, the water seeks the path of least resistance. Since it tends to travel in a given direction until it meets resistance, the channel on the outside of a bend (Point H) tends to be deeper, faster and less obstructed than the inside of the bend (Point I). You would like to stay in the outside channel, but you see a strainer in the water farther downstream (Point J).

So you decide to follow the outside channel partway and do an eddy turn at Point K — well upstream of the strainer. From there you can ferry across the river to the eddy at Point L, peel out and follow the route marked by the downstream Vs (Point M) to the bottom of the rapid.

Plan B: Self-Rescue Swimming

Suppose you zigged when you should have zagged, or worse yet, you leaned upstream and flipped over at the entrance to the rapid. Your brace failed and you couldn't roll, so you had to wet-exit. What do you do now?

Swimming in a rapid with all those rocks lurking around is a lot different than swimming in a pool. First things first: Figure out which way is downstream, then position yourself to float on your back with your feet downstream and your heels at the surface of the water (Fig. 6.6). It's much easier to push yourself away from a rock with your toes than with your nose, so keep your feet

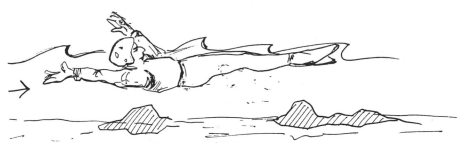

Figure 6-6
After wet-exiting in a rapid, try to keep your kayak downstream in front of you to minimize the risk of being pinned between it and a boulder. Float on the surface of the water with your feet downstream. Don't try to stand up!

downstream. And resist the temptation to "sit up" and look around you; that position drops your hind end down where it's sure to hit any rock in the vicinity. Make like an oil slick and stay on the surface of the water.

Don't try to stand up in moving water! A riverbed isn't a sidewalk. With so many rocks and irregularities, it's too easy for your foot to slip into a crack. This is called entrapment. With all the force of the current piling up on your leg, you wouldn't be able to pull your foot out of the crack. This is as much a hazard to be avoided as strainers and undercuts. Avoid entrapment by staying on the surface of the water.

Now what? You're floating downstream, and you know you don't want to float into that undercut or the hole or the strainer, and you're not wild about floating through all those rocks. Wouldn't it be nice to backferry over to a shoreline eddy and get out? Well, you can. The backferry can work as well without a boat as with one. Just angle the upstream end of your body (your head) the direction you want to go, backpaddle with your arms and kick with your legs. The current will push you toward the eddy (Fig. 6.7), where you can get out. (Actually, if there aren't a bunch of hazards just downstream, body ferrying like this is a lot of fun!)

But suppose there were no eddies above those hazards — no place to get out. (If this were true, you probably wouldn't have tried to run the upper part of the rapid.) You know you don't want to go into the undercut, so you choose the hole as the lesser of two

Figure 6-7
Body-ferrying is a way to self-rescue in the middle of a rapid.

evils. Some holes will flush you right through. Other holes can "recirculate" a swimmer. If that happens, try to stay as relaxed as possible. Catch a breath as the backroller brings you to the surface, then dive for the bottom and try to swim out along the riverbed.

Suppose you flushed through the hole and resumed the position of floating on your back with your feet downstream and your heels at the surface. There's still a strainer downstream. Ferry away from it! If, however, you someday find yourself swimming toward a strainer with no place else to go, here's what we recommend. Don't float into the strainer feet-first; you don't want your legs to get tangled in the branches and the current to push your head down. Instead, turn around and swim head-first aggressively toward the strainer; as you approach it, reach up as high as you can and pull yourself up on a branch. You may still be pinned by the force of the water, but at least you've done something to protect your ability to breathe until help reaches you.

Rescue Ropes
We think carrying and knowing how to use a rescue rope is a fundamental responsibility of every whitewater paddler. But while you should be prepared to offer help when needed, don't expect help to come to you. Paddle like you're all alone out there, and

avoid any situation where you would have to count on help to get you out of harm's way. It's each paddler's responsibility to use good judgment; it helps make the sport safer for everyone.

Suppose we return to the rapid we scouted in Fig. 6.5. Other members of your party are getting ready to run the rapid, but at your present skill level, you've decided to portage partway and put in downstream of the section with the hole and the undercut. You can set up a safety station to help out if a companion has trouble.

Get out your rescue bag (we described this in Chapter 1) and select a throwing position on shore. This position should be downstream of a potential tipover spot (preferably far enough downstream that a boater will have time to wet exit and get oriented to his surroundings before he floats past you), but upstream of hazards like undercuts, strainers and holes you wouldn't want to swim through. Also consider the pendulum factor: When a swimmer gets hold of that rope, he'll swing into shore like a pendulum. You don't want to swing him into a greater hazard; you want to swing him into a nice, safe eddy.

There are many regional and situational variations that affect rope rescues, but for now we'll just talk about the static belay. In this rescue, you consider all the position factors described above, plus one more: Pick a spot with good enough footing that after the throw you can plop yourself on the ground and dig in your heels so you can land your swimmer without getting pulled in yourself.

Open the neck of the bag a little more than halfway and pull out a length of rope. It there is a knot in the end of the rope (not the end tied to the bag — the other end), untie it. In a rocky riverbed, that knot can get wedged in a crack. Never set up a system that can't be released immediately if the rope gets tangled around some part of the swimmer's body. For the same reason, you never tie the rope to yourself or a tree or anything else.

Belay the rope around you, holding the bag in your dominant hand and gathering the rope in front of you with your other hand.

There are three ways to throw the bag — underhand, overhand and sidearm. Underhand throws tend to go straight up then fall straight down, hitting the water just a few feet from the thrower. And not everyone can throw the bag overhand like a football. Many people choose sidearm, which puts your whole body into the throw to give you the "oomph" to get the rope to the swimmer. No matter which throw you use, practice to gain accuracy.

Before you throw, try to get the swimmer's attention so he'll expect the rope and look for it; holler or whistle as loud as you can and try to make eye contact. Now, be patient. The most common problem people have is throwing too soon. Wait until the swimmer is just upstream of your position, and time your throw to land the rope (not the bag) in the "strike zone" between the swimmer's knees and eyes.

As soon as you release the bag, sit down and dig in. When the swimmer takes hold of the rope, you'll feel a strong tug. Hold onto your belay while the swimmer pendulums into the eddy. Don't try to "reel" him in; "saviors" have been known to pull the rope right out of the hands of their "savees". Stay dug in until the swimmer is in a secure position in the eddy.

If you're the swimmer, your first thought should be to look for the rope, not the bag; if you grab the bag and there's still rope in it, you won't pendulum toward the eddy until the rest of the rope has played out. When the rope lands in your strike zone, grab it and hold it over your shoulder and diagonally across your chest

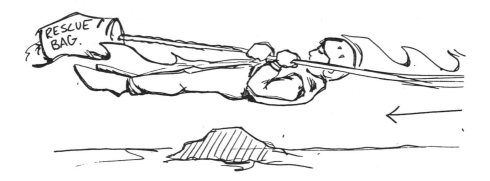

Figure 6-8
After getting a grip on things, pass the rescue rope to your outside shoulder. Voila — the angle you've set helps you ferry toward your rescuer as you pendulum toward shore.

without turning to look at the thrower (Fig. 6.8). If you just grab it and hold on, it will pull you over and water will ream your sinuses as you swing around. When you hold it over your shoulder, you'll plane across the surface and the water will plume up around your helmet instead of into your face.

If the rescuer gets a little excited and throws the rope a little too soon, swim for it or get ready to self-rescue swim. If the rescuer waits a little too long to throw, backpaddle with your arms and try to reach the rope or get ready to self-rescue swim.

Final Comments

This book is designed to introduce you to whitewater kayaking and to help you review techniques and principles you've learned. Since we can't be with you to answer your questions, clarify a pont, demonstrate skills, or reposition your body when you get twisted into a human pretzel, we urge you to get some coaching from a real, live professional kayaking instructor. Remember, practice doesn't necessarily make perfect, but it does make permanent. So if you're going to practice something, make sure you're doing it right. The best way to do that is with professional instruction.

Have fun as you practice the techniques described in this book. We hope it helps you learn to paddle safely, skillfully, confidently and with control. It's very satisfying to learn to do something well, but that's just one of the rewards of kayaking whitewater.

Whitewater paddling opens up opportunities for you to see some of the most beautiful, interesting and inspiring places on earth. Our rivers are living treasures. Each river, each rapid is unique and irreplaceable. Those of us who cherish them — paddlers, fishermen, property owners and others — have a responsibility to protect them. We can't afford to lose them.

Each eddy turn, each peel-out, each ferry in fast current, each moment in a rapid is a celebration of our rivers. We're glad you've joined the festivities. See you on the river!

INDEX